ABRICOTINE
The Imp Prince

BELLE
Beauty and the Beast

CINDERELLA
Cinderella

DONKEY-SKIN
Donkey-Skin

ELENA
The Frog Princess

FINETTE
Finette Cendron

GRETHEL
Hansel and Grethel

HANSEL
Hansel and Grethel

IMP PRINCE
The Imp Prince

JULEIDAH
The Princess in the Suit of Leather

KATIE WOODENCLOAK
Katie Woodencloak

LITTLE RED RIDING HOOD
Little Red Cap

MATCH GIRL
The Happy Prince

NUTCRACKER
The Nutcracker and the Mouse King

ONE-HANDED GIRL
The One-Handed Girl

PRINCE AIME AND PRINCESS AIMEE
The Orange Tree and the Bee

QUEEN OF THE FLOWERY ISLES
The Story of the Queen of the Flowery Isles

RAPUNZEL
Rapunzel

SNOW WHITE
Snow White and the Fox

THUMBELINA
Thumbelina

UGLY DUCKLING
The Ugly Duckling

VASILISA
Vasilisa the Beautiful

THE WHITE BRIDE
The White Bride and the Black Bride

XANTHE
Greek Mythology

YE XIAN
Ye Xian

ZEINEB
Princess Zeineb and King Leopard

Made in the USA
San Bernardino, CA
23 June 2015